In Spite of My Disability…

IN SPITE OF MY DISABILITY...

NORMA ASTORGA GARCIA

XULON PRESS

Xulon Press
2301 Lucien Way #415
Maitland, FL 32751
407.339.4217
www.xulonpress.com

© 2020 by Norma Astorga Garcia

All rights reserved solely by the author. The author guarantees all contents are original and do not infringe upon the legal rights of any other person or work. No part of this book may be reproduced in any form without the permission of the author. The views expressed in this book are not necessarily those of the publisher.

Printed in the United States of America.

ISBN-13: 978-1-6305-0299-7

Dedication

I want to dedicate this book to my mom and dad. They are the main people who pushed me and made me the resilient person that I am. I love you, and thank you for fighting for me against the doctor's advice.

To my loving husband Ozzy and my kids;

You have been the source of my inspiration, and you have filled my days with love and laughter. I love you all so much!

To my Lord Jesus Christ;

Thank you, Lord, for helping me all my life even when I did not know you were there. You have been my strength and my Rock during the challenging times. I pray that my story honors you and brings joy to others.

"By the grace of God, *I am what I am*," 1 Cor. 15: 10

Table of Contents

Chapter 1 The Struggle to Survive 1

Chapter 2 A New Found Hope 5

Chapter 3 Entering Mainstream Elementary 13

Chapter 4 My Middle School Years 21

Chapter 5 My Glory Years in High School 33

Chapter 6 Life-Changing Experience 43

Chapter 7 A New Beginning 47

Chapter 8 My Miracle Babies 51

Chapter 9 Raising My Kids 61

Chapter 10 New Opportunities 65

Closing 71

Chapter 1

THE STRUGGLE TO SURVIVE

I was born on October 15, 1971. It was a chilly evening out, and the autumn leaves were falling. My parents were Sergio and Ofelia Astorga, who already had two boys ages three and one. They lived in Matamoros, Mexico just 30 minutes South of Brownsville, Texas. My dad was heading out on a short trip to Houston that night when he forgot something and returned home. As he walked into the house, my mom told him she was having labor pains. Since they were from a low-class family, they went with a mid-wife in Brownsville. It was 10:30 pm, and my mother's labor went well, but as I came out, my umbilical cord wrapped around my neck. The mid-wife panic when she noticed the color of my body was purple. They decided to call the ambulance for help. It took about 10 minutes for the ambulance to arrive, but for my parents, it seemed like 30 minutes. Every minute is crucial when oxygen is not going into the brain. When the ambulance arrived, I received oxygen, and I was rushed to the hospital. The doctors at the hospital gave my parents no hope. They did not expect me to survive longer than three days. After the third day, I started responding to stimuli. The doctors, at this point, did not know the severity of the damage to my brain.

The official medical papers from the hospital stated my prognosis very bleak. I found a copy of this paper when I was 36 years old. Reading the doctors diagnosis made me realize the severity of my condition. This excerpt is from that form. ("Newborn white female born on 10-15-71 by a midwife and admitted to the hospital through the Emergency Room. Mother had been seen in my office for her prenatal, but the husband lost his job and went to a midwife. This time she was delivered of her baby, who had a prolapsed cord, and the infant was admitted to the ER being cyanotic and with shortness of breath and with convulsions, very lethargic and with weak reflexes. White female is well developed, and eyes are opened, pupils slightly dilated. Lips show cyanosis, the oral cavity is fair. Abdomen shows an umbilical cord tied with a string. The liver, spleen, and kidneys are not palpable. Reflexes are very weak, almost none. Baby cries spontaneously suddenly. Condition: Cerebral Anoxia, time of arrival: 11:45 pm"). ~After reading this now, I put myself in my mother's shoes' to imagine how she must have felt watching her newborn baby tremble uncontrollably. My tears came rolling down as I realized how pitiful I must have looked.~

My dad and my maternal grandmother decided to take us home and not tell my mother about any possible brain damage. They felt she need to recuperate from the delivery. Mom needed to go home to recover from the labor and enjoy her baby girl. My dad named me Norma after a well-to-do lady who had helped my grandparents in their time of need. My mom had her hands full with my oldest brother Sergio who was three years of age, my other brother Rick, was one year, and me a newborn. They lived a regular life until I was eight months old. My mom started wondering why I had not been able to sit. She thought it was a lack of attention because she was so busy at work and felt she was neglecting her duties as a mother to me. She finally convinced my dad to take me for a check-up. In those years, it was not mandatory for a regular check-up unless something was wrong. During the visit, the doctor noticed the lack of strength in my upper body and two clenched fists. The doctor did some tests on me and diagnosed me as having Cerebral Palsy. This condition is mainly caused at birth, although it can happen later in life with head trauma. It is caused due to a lack of oxygen to the brain and affects different areas of the brain. The severity of the condition depends on the amount of time the brain starves for oxygen.

My mom was devastated to hear the sad news and cried for a couple of days. She struggled from time to time with the thought that I would be 100% dependent on her for the rest of her life. She was already a quiet lady, but this news made her even more introvert. There were no support groups at the time to help parents work through the emotions associated with having a child with disabilities. Hispanics felt the stigma of having a disabled child because society sees the child as weak and unimportant.

Chapter 2

A New Found Hope

At the age of three, my parents moved to Brownsville, Texas. They bought their first house, and they were informed about free services for disabled kids. My parents went to Moody Crippled Children Clinic, which was a fantastic clinic that helped parents and their kids deal with a disability. I had to receive physical therapy, occupational therapy, and speech therapy. Mary Romaine gave me physical therapy. It entails mastering movements like walking, sitting, and standing. Mary was an older gentlewoman who always gave 110% of her effort to help you. At first, it is hard and frustrating, but she was continually encouraging. Rosie Medina was my occupational therapist. Rosie was a young new graduate filled with new ideas. Rosie used every opportunity to incorporate devices to assist me in feeding and dressing. She even helped me to think of different ways to perform my everyday care needs. Her methods are still part of my daily life, and I am grateful to her. My speech therapist, Debbie Sears, was also young and very beautiful. During our sessions, we would read books, look at picture puzzles, and play games with our mouths. My favorite exercise was when Debbie would put peanut butter on the inside of my cheek to manipulate my tongue. Little did I know this would help me develop the ability to speak. Therapy took patience and hard work, which my parents always taught me to do.

I am in Moody Clinic trying to learn how to tie my shoes.

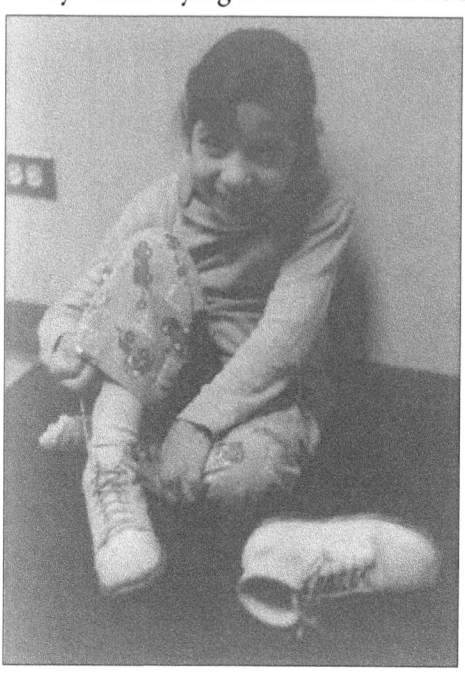

I attended a segregated school for the disabled adjacent to the clinic from Pre-K to second grade. There were all types of disabilities and abilities here. I have fond memories of laughter and sharing. I never experienced any discrimination from the staff. My first teacher was Margene Frazier. She was a short funny blond lady who loved children. I learned valuable life lessons and made long-lasting friendships. My last teacher in this school was and still is very special to me; her name was Debbie Olivares. She was a tall, beautiful green-eyed lady who loved helping others. She took me under her wing and supported me through high school. She spent extra work hours with me and got special equipment or permission for me to do certain things. She did this so I could feel just like any other student. After all that therapy, I finally learned to walk at seven years of age. Walking gave me a new sense of freedom to express myself. I will be eternally grateful to all these people because they impacted my life forever. ~ All three therapist ended up going to my wedding when I was 25 years old~

The two ladies on the right are my therapist, Mary, and Rosie.

The little skinny girl in the middle is me trying to use a shovel to plant a small tree.

There was not much information about people living with disabilities in the early '70s. My parents were too busy working or did not have the resources to find out what was available to me at the time. I was carried on my dad's shoulders everywhere we went before I was able to walk. We did not own a wheelchair since it was a luxury. He was never ashamed or embarrassed to be seen carrying his lanky six-year-old daughter even when people stared at him. He was proud of holding his beautiful little girl, according to him. He always got tired, but the joy of watching me have fun would give him the strength to take me where I wanted to go. I felt secure in his arms, and I knew he would be there to carry me when I needed him.

    I had several family members and friends who also encouraged me early on. My maternal grandmother (Abuelita Reyes) would come with us to the beach and take me out into the deep. She must have been 40 or 45 years old, but she was strong enough to hold me up from under my arms and fight the waves. The water would reach my chest; however, when the waves came, Abuelita would lift me to jump over them. The jumping movement was both fun and therapeutic.

    I have always considered myself a beach bum. I love the roaring sound of the ocean and the splashing of the waves. The whole beach scenery gave me peace in my heart. As I lifted over the mighty waves, it gave me a sense of happiness. On the other hand, this jumping and pushing off with my legs was a form of exercise. It would strengthen my leg muscles for better support on my walking and in some way, gave me self-confidence. As for me, this was a fun, intimate time with my Abuelita. My aunt Rosie also showed me lots of love and tender care that I knew I could always count on her. Another person who encouraged me was my aunt Estela. She would make fun of the way I walked. The negative comment may sound terrible; however, it became beneficial to me. As I started to walk, I would thrust my arms back to get a better balance, and my head would tilt to one side. My aunt would tease me that I looked like an airplane. This comment would seem harmful for many kids to hear, but for me, it made me want to improve myself and try harder.

My mother is encouraging me as I balance myself to take a step.

During those years, the Moody Clinic staff took a large group of disabled kids to the beach in the summer. Thinking back, this was a significant commitment to the staff. They were about five adults and at least 15 kids. The majority of them were quadapalygic, and some of us needed assistance in feeding. We would stay two nights at an oceanside motel with a kitchenette. Our parents dropped us off at the clinic Friday after work, and the staff; (Ms. Romaine, Debbie, and Rosie) drove us in their cars. They cooked dinner for us and got us ready for the night. The process did not merely mean to put our pajamas and get us into bed. It was more specific work. After feeding most of us, they fed those with feeding tubes. Next, they had to brush all of our teeth and change us into pajamas. The boys slept in one room and girls in another room. On Saturday morning, the whole process repeated itself for breakfast and every meal. We finally hit the beach after breakfast. Everybody was in their bathing suits, trying to push the heavy wheelchairs on the sand. I had a blast of fun! I loved the sounds of the ocean and playing on the sand. We all had a good time that even the staff got in the water to play. Nobody wanted to go back into the rooms to eat lunch, so they made sandwiches to eat by the sea. I think we stayed on the beach until late afternoon. The poor tired and exhausted staff had to come in to bathe all of us, change us, and cook for us. Once they put us into bed, they had a chance to shower and flop into bed. I did not realize then, but it must have taken determination and love for us kids to put themselves through all that hard work. There was no extra pay or extra recognition except the joy of making us happy. Sunday morning came with a dread. It was time pack up and clean-up so we could leave. On the way out, they treated us at Pizza Hut to end the trip. For the staff, it was time to go home to clean up, wash their clothes, and get ready for the next workday. It did not matter how exhausted they might have been; they always showed up to work with a smile. As for me, these trips made me feel independent from my parents for a while, and it would draw my friendships with my therapist even closer.

Debbie, my speech therapist, after a 25-year reunion, when she retired from The Mood Clinic.

I still remember the day I went to the bathroom by myself. We were at home, and my mom was very busy cleaning, so I went to the toilet and pulled down my pants. The seat was low enough for me to sit down. I then grabbed the paper and wiped myself, holding the paper with my thumb. I was so happy that I called my brothers to come and see my accomplishment. I felt very proud of myself because it meant one less thing I had to depend on mom. Even at this early age, I knew that it must have been hard for mom to care for my every need on top of her other responsibilities.

It was around 1978, when Brownsville school district enforced a law to mainstream disabled students into the public schools. I was among the first group of disabled children sent to regular schools. The change in law was an exciting time for my teachers and me. It was an experimental year to see if disabled students could fit in physically and academically with the rest of the students. The school district needed to see how disabled students would do given the same level of instructions. I felt proud of doing this and took the challenge seriously. I knew this was our chance to shine.

To qualify for the public schools, we had to take an aptitude test. I was excited, and I wanted the approval of my teachers. On the day of the testing, I was put in a small room on a one to one basis. The test seemed to last at least 4 hours. As the teacher and I came out of that room, I had confidence I had done well. I walked into the next room where my classmates were, and all of a sudden, I felt pressure in my head. I collapsed, and my body started to seize. I could not talk or move, but I was alert and heard everything. I was always joking and making people laugh. My classmates laughed at me because they thought I was pretending. I saw things like in a slow-motion movie. When this was over, I was terrified and started to cry.

I was rushed to the hospital to get checked. Doctors gave me a test called EEG. This test was to measure the electrical signals of the brain wave activity. If there are high spikes of electrical signals on the graph, it is an indication of a seizure. For a 7-year-old, it is a scary situation. They scrap small dots all around the scalp and put a gel-like substance in the same area. Then they put long wires hooked onto a tight cap connected to a machine. I was so scared because it seemed like this machine would give me an electric shock. For some reason, putting on this cap made me feel humiliating.

After the doctor diagnosed me with an epilepsy disorder, it took about two years to control it. Thankfully during this time, I only had about six seizures. It was hard for the doctors to find the right combination of anti-seizure medicine. Some medicine did not help me at all, and others would make my gums bleed every time I brushed my teeth. The medication also made my teeth crooked. Thankfully, my teeth straighten out on their own once the doctors figured out the right medicine. My poor mom had to take me to all of my appointments, and thus, she had to ask for time off from work. I'm sure it was stressful for her at work to take all that personal time off. As time passed, I could feel when a seizure was coming on. I felt my legs getting shaky and my head sensing pressure. I knew I had to lie down and wait for my whole body to stop shaking. When it was all over, I would cry in my parents' arms and be comforted by them. But then I would be fearful of the next seizure, not knowing when the next one would come again. I did not know, at the time, that I never had a so-called Grand Mal Seizure. Grand Mal seizures can be very violent and hurtful to the body. My seizures only lasted between 1 to 3 minutes. They were not so frequent. I could have a seizure once every four months or longer. The doctor considered it safe for me to go to school.

Chapter 3
Entering Mainstream Elementry

I entered the second grade at Russell Elementary. My mom was so afraid of this move that she insisted on me repeating this grade. My teacher was Mrs. Rocha. She had so much compassion that during recess, she would lift me by my underarms to help me run after the kids. It was hard to fit in sometimes, but I never let that stop me. I had terrible stares, ugly comments, and rejection; however, I always mustered the courage to go on. I was able to keep up with the schoolwork. I had to rely on fellow student's class notes for my study guide. At this early age, I always had determined to study hard and get good grades. I thought that if I had high grades, the kids at school would not reject me by thinking that I was also mentally disabled.

My days at school were full of excitement and new friendships. The only problem was that I could not feed myself efficiently yet. My mother, being a factory worker, had to ask for one hour off for lunch to go to my school everyday and feed me and then rush back to work. The monotony must have taken a significant toll on my mom, but there was no type of assistance from the school at that time. Every afternoon I would do all of my homework in my room. It took me twice as long because I had to work on homework plus any unfinished school work.

I know my mother struggled emotionally and physically with my disability; however, she never complained. Her self-esteem was low because she felt a stigma of not producing strong and healthy babies, in the Hispanic culture, it is vital. Mom was always caring for my needs when she was home, along with doing her other house chores. I am sure that by the end of the day, she was exhausted. Since both of my parents worked all day, there was always a maid at home to care for me. I had a normal childhood. I was treated equally with my brothers to do house chores and other responsibilities. I was also disciplined the same by getting a belt whooping when I deserved it. I acted like a tomboy at home. My two older brothers liked to wrestle, so I too would join in to wrestle with them at full force. My secret weapon in defending myself was to hit with my bonny elbow. I would fall full force with my body to hurt them with my elbow. I behaved very naughty with my middle brother Rick. We would pick fights at each other for no reason. My older brother Sergio (Checo) was always my savior when things got too rough with Rick. My father worked at a lumberyard, and my mother worked at a jean factory. We had enough food to eat, clothes to wear, and a house to live in, but my parents wanted more for us.

It was time for third grade, and things became more manageable for me. I was able to feed myself now. I had worked so hard all summer to master it. I did not want to put mom through that hassle again. I also felt embarrassed having mom feeding me in front of my friends. Mrs. Flores was another great teacher. She worked with me on one to one basis. She had me dictate to her many of my test answers so I can finish with my classmates. My handwriting was legible enough, but it took me long to write. I still kept going to the Moody clinic twice a week for all my therapies. I had built strong bonds with my therapists that I enjoyed going there. I had made close friends at school that I talked on the phone a lot and had plenty of sleepovers like a normal girl.

The house we lived in had three bedrooms with a patio and a carport. My mom liked gardening, so she always had the front lawn full of roses and other plants. Although she worked many hours, she would find time for her planting. Taking care of flowers and talking to them made her release stress and have a quiet time alone. The bedrooms were small but cozy. My room had the old fashion white with pink panels that made it look girly-like. I was a wrestling fan like my brothers, and thus, I plastered wrestling posters on my walls. A typical Sunday morning was to wake up, watch wrestling matches while eating breakfast, and go to church. My favorite wrestler was Kerry Von Eric because he had long hair and was charismatic.

Fourth grade came with excitement because my teacher was known as a dance instructor. Many girls thought he was handsome and a well-dressed man. Schoolwork was challenging, but I managed with the help of my brothers. I was in love with love itself, and somehow I always manage to have a crush on a boy. I had a couple of close friends to share my thoughts and ideas. My mom would find time to take my friends and me to the mall or out to eat. I was an extravert! I was able to make friends easily and be loved by all the teachers.

During the summer of 1979, my dad managed to open his own lumber company. I do not know all the details of how he did this, but he did. My dad, a Mexican citizen and with only a sixth-grade education, manage to get a loan from the bank to open Astorga Lumber Yard. The store was located on Fronton St. near the International Bridge into Mexico. The location was good because we got plenty of Mexican business. My mother quit her secure job to join forces with my dad. It must have been a terrifying journey; however, they were willing to risk it all for a better future. My brothers were encouraged to help in the lumber yard. Checo was 12 years old, and Rick was ten years old. They were a big help in spite of their young age. I remember my dad staying late at work while mom would come home to get us ready for bed. My mother only had a seventh-grade education with plenty of manual labor in her work history. Somehow, they figured out how to do the accounting books and the order forms to buy all the materials for the business. My parents had some knowledge to speak English; however, it was still very raw at a basic level.

I am proudly wearing my dad's lumber yard shirt after the grand opening of his business.

Fifth grade came and went without a hitch. Mrs. Hodges was kind but strict. Her energetic teaching habits reinforced my attitude in my work. I disciplined myself to do all my homework first before getting on the phone or doing any other activities. I kept being an A-B student while still having fun. Some of my friends' names were: Hercillia, Gloria, Rose Anne, Beatriz, and many more. They were all from different walks of life. It did not matter to me if they were rich or poor; they were my friends. Boys were in the picture, of course. We would all play and tease each other at the playground.

This summer was fun. My parents' lumber yard was slowly taking off. My brothers worked part of the summer with my dad. I stayed home most of the time. A regular summer day for me was to wake-up by 10 am, eat breakfast by 11 am, and spend the rest of the day watching TV. I was never into reading books; however, I would force myself to read one small book the whole summer. When Rick was home, it was a constant battle with him. We are one year apart, so that made it very comparative. We would pick fights with each other out of boredom. I picked up a good habit. My brothers liked break-dancing music and practiced the dance moves often. I liked slow romantic music and decided to start recording radio songs onto cassette tapes. It took hard work and precise timing to end the recording on the right note. My first 45-inch record was the song "Funky Town." I kept recording and buying records. I enjoyed songs mostly from the '60s and '70s. I am a hopeless romantic. My favorites singers were: Elvis, The Beatles, Hall & Oats, and my number one singer is Berry Manilow.

My '81-'82 sixth grade was full of challenges. All of us were getting older. We started to take an interest in the opposite sex, and this year represented the end of elementary school. I had mixed emotions at the beginning of this year. I was 11 years old, and my body started to bloom. I had long legs that made me look tall for school pictures. My breasts also started to show. My early development was a bit of concerned for my mom. She secretly had wished that my body would not have bloomed in this early stage of my life to avoid having any problems with teasing. The boys started to look cute and exciting. I longed to have a boyfriend just like the other girls. I would see the couples holding hands or meeting each other at the movies, and that made me wonder when it would be my time. I went out to the movies and to the mall with my girlfriends to socialize and sometimes we met up with a group of boyfriends to talk. Even though I longed for a boyfriend, it never affected my personality. I was always a positive, easy-going girl. In private, I may have gotten sad, but I tried to look happy around people.

In the first week of school, the school announced that we had a new P.E. coach. As we went to P.E., all the girls were amazed at how attractive this man was. He fit the cliché: tall, dark, and handsome. His name was Mr. Padilla, and he was 23 years old. He had a great personality that made him get along with all the teachers. When it was time for my grade to go to P.E, most girls wanted to be first in line to reach the coach first. It sounds exaggerated, but it is true. I even heard teachers talking about how handsome he was. The principal had a daughter in my grade, so she became my greatest rival to get the coach's attention. Her name was Marisol. She was short and chubby. Since her mother was the principal, Marisol felt like she had special privileges. She was rough and stern and always wanted to be first at every game. Coach Padilla treated everyone with respect and kindness, no matter who you were. I'm sure he noticed many little girls had a crush on him. He was very respectful to that matter.

When my birthday came around, he gave me a brown teddy bear with a yellow bow around its neck. I was thrilled knowing he took the time to buy me the teddy bear. He told me that his wife helped him pick it out. I went home and slept with that bear every night for that whole year because I was proud to have something more special than the rest of the girls. I met his wife later that year. She would come to special events at my school. Julie was the kindest and loveliest lady I had met. I kept in touch with them for two more years after elementary. ~ Twenty years later, our friendship in elementary school became an educational time for them. They now had three kids, and the youngest had Cerebral Palsy like me. Their pain of finding this out was not too hard since they remembered how much I was able to do. I was able to tell them about my childhood and encouraged them about their daughter's development. ~

Summertime came very quickly. I was having so much fun in school, and I was not looking forward to saying good-bye to some classmates who were going to another school. My parents' lumberyard was booming. We had just had a big hurricane hit the southern tip of Texas. All lumber companies and groceries stores near the ocean sell out when there is a hurricane warning. People rush to protect their houses and stock up on food. After the hurricane hit, some people had to repair or rebuild their homes. My dad earned a considerable profit after the storm recovery. He was able to pay off all his debt and invest in new things.

My friends and I kept on going to the mall, movies or having slumber parties. During this era, it was safer to leave young teenagers at the mall and not worry about kidnapping or any other violent crimes. My mom would drop off my friends and me at the mall, and she would pick us up

Entering Mainstream Elementry

later. Mom always knew who my friends were and their parents. My parents gave me trust in return for good behavior. I honored the trust and the freedom they gave me. I now think back on how hard it must have been for my parents to let me go out alone with friends. Though they did help me, I was pretty self-sufficient. I walked and talked well enough to keep up with the other girls.

Towards the end of summer, mom took my brothers, my friend Hercilla, and me to a water park at South Padre Island, which was only 30 minutes away from my home. It was a whole day of adventure. We rode on the water slides for a couple of hours. The day was exhausting for my mom because she had to support me up the stairs to all the water slides and slide down with me to lift me out of the water at the end. My mom was determined to make me happy, no matter the cost to her because my happiness was her happiness! After this, we went to ride the bumper cars. Hercilla and I rode together while we raced against my brothers. I'm sure the whole day was costly, but it was a wonderful treat after working so hard at the lumberyard. ~I did not recognize it then but looking back I see how courageous and loving my mom was to me.~

My mother was helping me up the long path to get up on the water slide.

Chapter 4
My Middle School Years

It was time to go back to school. I was entering 7th grade at Stell Junior High School. I had mixed feelings knowing some friends had to go to a different school because they belonged to another zoning area, and that made me sad. The idea of going to a bigger school and having many more people to meet made it thrilling. I liked the challenge of introducing and developing new friendships. It was exciting but yet scary of that initial rejection. Because of my speech, I held back meeting people the first time I saw them. I would first observe someone who I wanted to meet to understand their personalities or attitudes. Then, I would muster up the courage to talk to them about their interests. The more nervous I felt the worse my speech would do. However, I knew that was one part of my life that I had to overcome.

    I started my '83-'84 school year. The night before school, I could not sleep at all. I was very excited and wondered which new outfit I would wear. Mom dropped me off at the school office, and from there, someone took me to my homeroom. It had been decided, with the administration, that I would leave each class 5 minutes early to go to my other class to avoid the trampling of all the students in the hallway. The procedure was a good idea, but for me, it felt like I was losing out in all the socializing. After a while of doing this, I would leave my backpack in my next classroom and stand outside in the hallway, watching the other students interact. It was fun for me, waving and saying hi to the students while keeping a safe distance. It did not take long for the whole junior high to recognize me and know my name since I was the only disabled student there who later became very active. I wanted to get involved with the school activities as much as I could. I decided to join the pep-squad.

The pep-squad was a group of girls who helped the cheerleaders chant the cheers louder from the stands. I thought this was an excellent opportunity to be involved in something without sticking out too much. My childhood neighbor, Becky, joined the pep-squad with me. We were inseparable! We also joined the Student Council club. It was great. My parents knew we were together, so that meant to them that I was safe no matter where we were. I got used to the routine of going back and forth to all my classes. The interaction with the other kids gave me the confidence to walk around the school with my head up. Being in the pep-squad made me look forward to Saturday morning's football games to have fun.

Me, on the far left, chanting the cheers with my pep-squad..

By October, my dad took a big step of faith and bought a new house for us. The house had five big bedrooms, five restrooms, two living rooms, one dining room, a wet bar, a large kitchen, and a washroom. If that was not enough, it had a workout room, a large backyard with a lake adjacent to it with a gazebo on top of the lake. Being at the gazebo, it felt like heaven to me because seeing the water in the lake and feeling the wind on my face made me feel peaceful. I also had French doors from my bedroom to the lake. My room was very dainty with pink flowers all around. We were so happy with our house that we could not wait to have company over.

I was enjoying my school activities with Becky. I was sad that we were not neighbors anymore, but we hung out with each other at school. The 7th-grade student council was looking for a place to host their Christmas party; hence, I gladly offered my house. My mom and I were extremely excited about putting up the holiday decorations. The sponsor for the student council was my math teacher Mrs. Benavidez. She was an intelligent and very outgoing teacher. She taught Algebra in such a way that it made me understand it and love it. ~This party was the first of many parties I would have throughout the years.~ My good friend Hercillia and other friends from elementary were also in this club. In the spring semester, the student council took us on a trip to Houston to visit the NASA Space Center. My parents let me go without them. I was even more self-efficient to be by myself with some help from friends. During all this, I was still doing the pep-squad for the football season and then for the basketball season. I had tremendous fun fitting in and just being one of the girls. My grades were A-B average with an occasional C. I worked on my homework every night for 3 hours.

In spite of all the fun I was having, I still longed to be a cheerleader. Somehow my friends talked me into trying out in front of the whole student body. My mom, of course, tried to talk me out of it to keep me away from any humiliation. I was nervous, scared, and shy in a way; however, this was something I had been thinking of doing for a while. I had to practice every day after school, and I campaigned for my votes.

On the morning of the try-outs, my mom sat in the crowd to watch me do my cheer. I was excited and full of nerves, but at the end of my cheer, I received a standing ovation. A friend told me that she saw my mom wiping off tears from her eyes. I believe those were tears of accomplishment. The front office announced the winners through the intercom. After they said my name, my class cheered for me. I was overwhelmed! My dream was coming true. After school, teachers and students were congratulating me in the halls. The sense of accomplishment gave me a boost of self-esteem. Becky and I ended up appearing in the yearbook at least four times with all the clubs and activities we did around the school. My favorite picture was when Becky and I dressed up for Punk Day during our spirit week. We tore our clothes, we teased our hair, and we did our make-up like a punk rocker. Sure, it was scary and embarrassing to think that no one else would dress the part, but I wanted to show my school spirit. In our last week of school, we got to sign each other's yearbooks, and mine was full.

Becky and I dressed up for Punk Day.

I did not like the summer. Summer felt like a long time without interacting with all of my friends, but then it was a time of relaxing without homework. My parents started to take time off from the lumber yard. We went on our first family trip to Disney Land in June of '83. It was a memorable trip. We went to Disney Land, Escott Center, and Notts Berry Farm. I can walk on my own; however, walking and standing in lines for long periods got me very tired. Disney Land was the first place where they told us that at any theme park, disabled people should be accommodated to go right up to the front of the lines for the rides. After this, we rented a wheelchair and took advantage of the policy. My brothers loved using me to get on rides over and over. Since my brothers liked big and scary rides, I had to be brave to go up with them to be in the front of the line. Most of the rides sit two persons; therefore, my mom had to ride with me and hold me while I had the time of my life. My mom must have been in her early 40's, but now I know that it is around that age when you stop going on high roller coasters.

The rest of the summer, I spent my days going to cheerleading practice at school. It was decided by the sponsor that I would be the school mascot since the group needed all cheerleaders to be able-bodied to perform the cheerleading pyramids. It did not bother me a bit. I was happy to be part of that group and wear the same uniform. It was hard at times because the more dedicated girls did not feel I fit the image of a cheerleader. I had set my mind to prove them wrong. I would sit in my room practicing the cheers over and over until one day I recorded myself chanting those cheers. I had received an opportunity to do something I had dreamed of, and I wanted to give it my best.

My mom did give me some opposition in being the mascot for fear of me getting physically and emotionally hurt. The laughing at me by other students' or the possibility of me tripping and falling in front of the crowd made my mom worried, but I assured her I was willing to give it a try. In my head, I knew I could not give up.

The start of my 8th-grade year '84-'85 came with high expectations. We all felt superior to the 7th graders, and it was my time to shine. Becky and I still stayed involved with as many school clubs we could handle and even kept good grades. The point to this was to make as many friends as possible to fit in with the in-crowed. Football season started, and I was busy every Saturday morning cheering for our team. There were times when we had to travel to other towns for outside games. It was exhilarating for me to go away for a school function without my parents. My squad always looked out for me in case I needed any help. I tried to ask for the least amount of help so that nobody could feel that I was a burden and hence think that I do not belong there. I never wanted anyone to have that impression of me or feel sorry for me. I knew I needed to overcome any obstacle for my self-worth. Most people have the misperception of disabled persons also being mentally slow. The perception is not always the case. We can have a physical challenge, a mental challenge, or both combined but not necessarily. It depends on the degree of severity the brain was affected by the loss of oxygen. Fortunately, my brain was not severely affected as not to understand basic instruction or to pick up on social cues from people. My level of intelligence has been to par with the rest of my peers.

I am cheering with my cheerleading squad.

One day I went to a football player's party with Becky, and it was a disaster. It was my first party with the football players and with the in-crowd that I felt proud and happy to be with the gang. My mom dropped us off even without knowing who lived at the house. The notion may seem a little scary now, but back then, it was still reasonably safe to drop off your kids at a friend's house without going in and meeting the parents. The party started fine with sodas and snacks, but later, alcohol and regular cigarettes began to show up. I was not alarmed by this because alcohol and cigarettes were an average substance but of course, still illegal to minors. Any drugs, on the other hand, I did not want any contact. My parents had already installed in my mind to stay away from all drugs, and I did not want to damage my brain even more. As the party went on, pot cigarettes started to pop up too. Some people in the party were smoking the pot in the house, so the neighbors would not notice the smell. By doing this, all the smoke stayed in one or two rooms, so all of us at the party had to inhale it. After a while, we heard a police siren in the distance, and we all started running through the neighborhood. I could not believe I was doing this. If the police had caught me, I would be ashamed at something I did not even do. I did not want to ruin my family's business reputation with a stupid action like that. I did not need this trouble in my life. I called my brother Rick to come to pick up Becky and me from a side street where we ran after the police car drove by the house. I was back home safe with my friend Becky. My parents never learned about this incident.

Meanwhile, I would attend all the school dances or other activities going on at school. Although I had many friends, mom would drop me off alone and then meet up with my group of friends since my house was far from my school. Being dropped off alone can be a scary situation. What if my friends did not show up, and I was there without a close friend to rely upon? Since it was already hard for me to ask my friends for help, it was even harder to ask someone else for assistance. It was not because they would deny me or feel bothered by it, but it was mostly my pride that did not want people to think I was useless. Although this is how I thought, I quickly learned how to accommodate in any situation. Many students and teachers knew who I was from walking all around campus, so it made it easier to start a conversation.

My friend Gloria, who was the head cheerleader, invited some of the cheerleaders to stay at her parents' condo for the weekend. Since my parents and her parents knew each other, I got to go. I was very excited since I am a beach bum, and I was going to have an independent weekend. The days fun and filled with adventure. We would wake up late, walk out to the beach, and spend the whole day laying out sun tanning and talking about boys. When I was by the ocean, it made me feel free and close to God. I was still too young and not mature enough to know how to have a real relationship with God, but I did feel something special. We would then go back to the condo to watch movies and eat. I enjoyed the whole atmosphere of being at the beach, having a carefree attitude with a pleasant tan.

I would often daydream that if I ever got married, I would like to have a beachfront wedding and enjoy a beautiful and cozy beach house. I knew this was an unattainable dream of mine because I could not see anyone wanting to marry me. It was not that I would see myself as ugly or not fun to be around, but who would want to be responsible for a disabled woman when they can have so many options. My dad would sometimes try to encourage me that I will have a husband and possibly children to love. I figured my dad was trying to cheer me up. My thoughts did not mean I was hopelessly sad or depressed about my future, but I would not allow myself such high hopes to enter my mind. I thought I could be entirely happy with only having good friends by my side. I would much later find out how wrong this statement was.

Spring Break was always a long-awaited time of the year. It meant time off from school to relax and catch up with the soap operas. The city of Brownsville would get a plentiful amount of tourism from Winter Texans to Spring Breakers. The whole month of March would be full of people from all over the Country. My family spent time looking at the license plates to see from what State they were coming. It was a family pass- time we would do while driving around town. It was also funny to watch total strangers act dumb and irresponsible while being in my city. This year my whole mentality changed. Since I was 14 years old, reaching puberty, and being popular in school, I felt old enough to join the spring breakers.

Every week during Spring Break, the beach had different performers on stage. The week before I had the week off from school, Eddie Money was playing during school hours. He was very popular at this time, and I beg my parents to let me skip school so I can be at the concert. I do not know why my parents agreed on this, but I am glad they did! They probably said yes because perhaps they thought if they said no, I would still skip school and could be in harm's way. At this time, my dad had a gorgeous full figure young lady as a cashier at his lumber yard. Gracie was very outgoing and liked to joke around with the men at work. My mom deliberated up a good idea where each of us could be happy.

Our cashier Gracie would take me to the concert at the beach to have fun while still getting paid. The arrangement was an unbelievable deal for me because I could have an exciting story to tell and perhaps meet cute older guys with Gracie's looks.

My friends could not believe this arrangement and wished their parents would let them go with me. I felt honored my parents trusted me with this event. The day came for my 1st real spring break experience without mom and dad. On that day, we left in the morning to pick the right spot at the beach for the concert before the crowds came in. We managed to get a front stage space to hang out before the show started. As the day went by, the people began to arrive with their ice chests full of beer and getting wild and drunk. I had only seen this behavior from far away, and now I was caught in the middle of it. There were guys drinking beer non-stop. They were also drinking it upside down to get a faster buzz. I was impressed by the whole atmosphere, and yet it did not scare me. My hopes came true with Gracie in her bikini. Many groups of guys would flock around us, wanting to talk with her. I took advantage of this and spoke to the guys too. The experience shot up my self-esteem tremendously. I know it was all in my head, but it felt enchanting that cute guys wanted to be around me. The Spring Break adventure was the 1st of many Spring Break memories that I would have.

The next day at school, I was a big hit. I was showing off pictures and mementos of this incredible concert. I did, however, get in trouble at school. When I told them I had my parents' permission, they could not punish me. I felt my head growing full of pride; thus, it gave me my first taste of mischief.

As May was approaching, students started giving the end of the year parties. Of course, I hosted one at my house. There were endless amounts of food that mom would make herself with all kinds of goodies teenagers enjoy. My living room was huge, with a wooden floor that opened itself to become an excellent dance floor. We would dim the lights, crank up the cassettes, and start dancing. My parents were always in the house but stayed in their room. I guess they felt more comfortable knowing we were safe at home and not somewhere else, not knowing what we were doing. I do confess that at another party, I did get into a car where the driver was drunk. I knew what I was doing was wrong, and I could hear my parents' voices in my head warning me not to do this. I still did it because it felt fun, and I surrendered into peer-pressure. I can assure you this was not the last dumb thing I did, but thinking back, I know God's protection was over me.

During all my school years, I still kept going to the clinic for therapy on my hands and legs. They would teach me tricks and show me ideas on how to do something with my abilities. That means to use your hands or any part of your body differently to do a simple task. All these tricks would be useful in all areas of my life.

By now, I knew God had gifted me with an easy-going personality and an ability to adapt to any physical or emotional challenge. I believed that no one would look after me better than myself, so I decided to fight for everything I wanted to do.

The second half of the summer was spent practicing and preparing for my big event, my Quincenera. In the Hispanic tradition, this is a coming out of age celebration. It is like the Sweet 16th party but one year before. The ceremony is a huge party; nevertheless, my parents made it into an elaborate celebration. I did not know how big it would be until that day. I had to pick 14 girls and their partners to dance three songs. My brother, Checo, choreographed all the dance steps. It was difficult to gather 28 people all at the same time 1 or 2 times a week. It was fun getting together to goof around. We kept on doing this until October when the big event happened.

My parents, my brothers, and me during my Quincenera.

Chapter 5

My Glory Years in High School

My Freshmen year of high school '85-'86 was a brand-new start again. The halls were more significant, the people were taller, and my mind was full of possibilities. I felt so grown-up entering the high school that my mom took me to buy a whole new wardrobe to match my age. Even though I did not have Becky in the same school, I still looked forward to joining the school clubs. After the excitement wore off, I felt very intimidated by all the people that I did not know and who would not take the time even to acknowledge me. The awkwardness made me feel self-conscience and shy that I kept to myself. I still had my friends, but they got into sports or other activities that I could not do. The discomfort of the situation made me recluse to my books and study hard. I did have more homework than others since I was not able to finish classwork, I would take it home.

In early October, I finally had my Quincenera. It was a day many other people, and I would not soon forget. I had a hairdresser come to the house to do my hair and make-up. There were many caterers delivering food to the dance hall and flower shop drivers dropping off large amounts of arrangements. Once everything was ready, we headed to the church to have a one-hour mass to celebrate my coming of age. The procession looked beautiful. There were 14 girls dressed in hot pink ankle-high dresses and their partners dressed in black tuxedos. At the end of the line, I show up with a light pink beaded ballroom dress and my oldest brother on my side with a white tuxedo.

At the dance hall, we did two traditional slow dances plus a modern song called Venus. The crowd went wild when they heard this song because people were starting to break with tradition. We had a feast, and then the live band started. People danced to their hearts desired. There was then a 30 minutes intermission when the leader of the group performed impersonations of famous Mexican singers. I did not know of this surprise, but it was awesome. Later on, came an even bigger surprise. Once again, the leader of the band stepped onto the dance floor to lead a massive conga line. Then, all band members start to pass out can shape shakers. It was incredible how many people got up to join this line. There were about 500 people present, and I think at least 300 formed the line. We were shaking the cans with one or with both hands trying to make as much noise as possible. This dance lasted about 15 minutes, just going around every table and putting the spotlight on people. Yes, we did have these many people because my parents invited family, friends, and business acquaintances.

On Monday at school, all my friends were talking about my party and how much fun it was to be there. They even got the other kids interested in the details. All the positive comments made me feel like a queen for that day, knowing that people were talking good about me.

I had heard that in Mexico City, people would celebrate Christmas more traditionally. My parents had distant relatives that we would visit them at the Capitol of Mexico, and everyone got along great. The family had always invited us to go for the holidays, but of course, my parents had their business to run. I beg them to let me experience those beautiful traditions. To my amazement and excitement, I was able to go! I flew alone into the International Airport of Mexico City, where my relatives were waiting for me. I had a blast three weeks there visiting more relatives and experiencing all kinds of festivities. My mother flew in to bring me back home. ~ As an adult now, I can't believe my parents let me do that!

By the end of the school year, I qualified to be among the Who's Who Top 10% of the class. The ceremony we had was very fancy. All of the girls wore semi-formal dresses, and the boy dressed up nicely too. We all took turns in going up to the stage and receive our awards for a job well done. I felt out of place because this group of students was not the usual group of students I would hang out. These people were considered to be nerds, but I did not think of myself as a nerd. I did, however, enjoyed dressing up and getting attention on how I looked. My Freshman year would be the only year I would obtain achievement because it took too much of studying and commitment. I then got more interested in hanging out with friends than getting awards. Do not misunderstand me I still kept on getting an A-B maybe some C averages.

That is me in the middle of the picture with the top of the class students.

The next major event was at the end of my Sophomore year '88. Once again, I ran for the school mascot. I did tryouts and campaign for the votes. It was a more significant student body and more chances to lose, but something in me gave me the courage to go for it. I thought of all the possibilities and the fun it could bring. I did win again, and it was an enormous pride and honor I could ever have. That summer was full of practice and cheerleading camps. I still received some ugly stares and comments; however, that was not going to stop me.

'88-'89 My Junior year became my most memorable year ever. School classes were becoming fun because we were able to joke around with some of the teachers. We were not considered to be among the younger students anymore. I joined enough school clubs to keep me busy every morning and most afternoons with cheerleading practice. I had made close friendships with a group of 6 girls: Leah, Laura, Terry, Laura, Martha, and Penny. We were a close-knit group who would always sit together for lunch. They would go to the football games and hang out in the stance while I would be cheering out on the field. I had lots of fun being part of the cheerleaders, but I did miss hanging out with my real friends.

It is my Viking Mascot outfit.

One day at an away game, a news reporter saw me cheering. The encounter led the reporter to visit my school to interview me. I was called to the office to talk with the reporter. During the interview, I felt like I was on cloud nine! My story came out in the local newspaper with a picture of me cheering on top of another cheerleader's shoulders. Oh boy, how exciting that was for me! After the article came out, I started to get requests from local groups of people with disabilities to come and share my story with them. I only attended to two invitations to speak, but that started up my passion for encouraging kids and their parents on how to live victoriously with their disabilities.

I went on with my school activities having fun and growing in popularity with the in-crowd; however, I loved just hanging out with my small group of friends. Friday nights after the football games, we would eat at Burger King and stay there for hours laughing and wondering if the workers would ever kick us out. I saw my life as a typical teenaged girl, just like in the movies. I thought this was all I needed to be happy, but soon enough, I discovered how wrong I was.

Ever since 7th grade, I had known a boy named TJ, who had always caught my eyes. He was a tall, blonde, green-eyed football player. I had him for a couple of classes that year; nonetheless, it was a distant friendship. However, we mingled more with each other since we would meet at the football players' parties. We would hang out at the parties, tell jokes, and talk about the school games. All my friends knew about the big crush I had for TJ, and yet, they could not believe how close as friends we would act at the parties. I am pretty sure that by now, he had an idea of how I felt about him. I never told him or acted in such a way to show him that I liked him. It was fun to be considered to be one of the guys and to fit in the in-crowd. Every time I saw him walking down the hallway, I would get butterflies in my stomach and get a nervously laugh. My friends knew without looking who was approaching by my behavior. I had other crushes with other boys, but this was my main guy.

It was near Valentine's Day, and the Student Council was planning their dance. This year they had made a special rule for the dance. The girl would ask the boy to be her date for the night. The announcement was music to my ears. When I heard the rules for the dance that day, my heart raced, and I thought this was my only chance to go out with Tj on an actual date. Although I had been to many school dances with guy friends in a group, I still had never been on a one-to-one date before. I knew I had to hurry up to ask TJ to go to the dance with me before any of the more popular girls ask him first. By now, he was a well-known football player and loved by others. I mustered all the courage I had and asked him flat out. To my surprise, he said yes! In my mind, I was yelling and jumping for joy, but on the outside, I played it cool. When I told my friends what I did, they were ecstatic for me. I had two weeks to prepare and daydream of my date.

On the day of the dance, I was so excited and ready for the date. I spent the whole day smiling and wishing that moment was already here. I even worried that TJ could stand me up at the last minute. When I heard my doorbell ring, I got butterflies in my stomach. He came in, and he looked very handsome dressed up. As we walked to the car, he told me we are double- dating with a close friend of his. That was fine with me. I just wanted my time with TJ. The dance was great. He was like most boys that age who do not know how to dance, but I forced him to dance. We also took the traditional school dance pictures. It was a great night for me, and it was a night to remember. Our relationship after that was of good close friends.

It was time for the Prom dance, and my brother Rick was planning his Prom date. The Prom was usually for Seniors,' but they did let some Juniors attend. I wanted to go, so I asked my brother Rick's friends to go with me. Julio was a hilarious guy that kept everyone laughing, and I thought I could not go wrong with that. Mom took me to buy a peach ballroom dress with an elegant matching hat that looked like from the '60s. I was ready to impress anyone. We double-dated with my brother and his date, and the night was full of laughs and dancing. Since I was with Rick, I did not have a curfew because I was in safe hands with him. Little did mom know that Rick was showing me the nightlife. After the dance was over, we sneaked into a club to dance some more. My mom was an early sleeper, so whenever we got home from being out, we just peeked into their bedroom to announce that we made it back. In the morning, she would not remember what time we got back. I learned how to hide my late arrivals by pretending I was with my brothers.

We had live-in help with us for eight years, and her name was Vicenta. She was a short, sweet, quiet mannered older lady who liked serving us. Whatever we needed, she was always ready to do it. On the nights I would come home late, she would also cover up my late arrival by telling mom I got there earlier. She became my confidant. We talked about boys I liked or about what other girls were doing. She became a great help and a friend to all members of my family.

My brother Sergio had started attending our local college and was involved in some social clubs. As he made friends and hanged out with members of these clubs at my house, my brother introduced me to some of these friends. I would get a sense of excitement when I was talking to older guys while I was still in high school. I felt like I had something above all the other girls. Sergio also offered our house to host some parties, and of course, I was there to benefit from it. I noticed how different older guys talked to me. They seemed to have some sense of direction about their lives. They still acted foolishly and liked to party; hence, this was what attracted me the most. I felt all grown-up going back to school and telling my friends about the parties I would go to with my brothers. Towards the end of my Junior year, they had announced the new try-outs for next year's mascot, but I decided not to run. I wanted to feel free to go hang out with my buddies.

Summer '89 was a fantastic time for me. Dad took the 5 of us on a seven days cruise ship to Hawaii. Mom and I, of course, had to buy new clothes to go on this trip. The cruise is when I purchased my 1st decent bikini, not knowing that there would be many more to come with less material. The big day of our flight arrived, and emotions were running high before getting on the plane. We had a 7 hours flight with movies to watch and a fee meal to eat. Arriving in Hawaii, greeters received us with a lay. The trip was so beautiful because we went around all the islands and we even saw an irrupting volcano. We walked on a white sand beach and also stepped on hot lava. The remarkable scenery with exotic flowers and fresh vegetation blow my mom's mind away. My favorite part of the trip was on the ship itself. It had life 24 hours a day. We had hula dance classes, mid-night buffets, pools, and an ocean view to remember. I did not want to go back home at all because I loved being around God's beauty. After this, we had plenty of pictures to show off to family and friends.

The start of my Senior year was with great anticipation. My friends and I knew we were going to rule the school year. It was our last year; therefore, we had to make it memorable. We hung out at every football game, went out to eat, and attended the football players' parties. Those parties kept on getting crazier and crazier. All that peer-pressure to keep up with all the drinking to stay with the in-crowd was always there. Yes, idiot me, I wanted to show off that I was also one of the guys, so I drank. We all know how teenagers can be encouraging others to do something they usually would not do.

At school, some teachers gave the seniors special treatment down the hallways or in a class by talking to us and not at us. Teachers would let us walk in the halls without asking for a permission slip. They were also getting us ready to take the SAT's and advising us for college. The planning of our academic future seemed exciting and nerve-wracking, realizing we were about to become adults in the real world and make our own decisions. My principle decided to get me a letter man's cheerleader's jacket even though I was not in the cheerleading squad this year; as a result, that created bad comments among the current cheerleaders saying that I did not deserve a jacket. After some bickering, I was grateful for getting a jacket to feel part of the letter man's senior group.

My senior Prom was awesome. My date was a college friend of my brother. I had known Danny for about a year. He was energetic, funny, and very charming. My friends already knew of him, but they were very shocked that I had invited him to prom. My friends and I had rented a limousine to drive four couples to the Prom. We all met at my house while we waited for the limo. We took pictures and recorded silly videos of ourselves. Driving in the limo was an experience in itself. The girls had our long ballroom dresses while the boys looked good in their tuxedos. The dance was a blast! We danced all night. I was showing off my date and took lots of pictures to remember this night. After Prom, my girlfriends spent the night at my house. Even though my parents were sleeping in the house, I still managed to misbehave by drinking in there. We had snuck a bottle of champagne to celebrate the end of an era. ~Thinking back now I feel so sorry I did that to my parents who always put their trust in me.~

My friend Danny and I ready to go to the Prom.

At the end of the school year, we had student council elections to vote among the student body who would be the most popular, most liked, etc. My Senior class voted me in for The Most Spirited of the year. Wow, I loved that nomination. My yearbook was full of signatures on the last day of school. It was a sad time because it was never going to be the same, no matter the close friendships.

The day of our graduation had finally come. It was June 4, 1990, and my emotions were full of excitement. I wanted to stand out even more besides from my disability, so I decided to put shiny metallic letters on top of my cap. The cap said, "I'm out of here." I did not know if this was allowed, but I figured they could not hold me back. Sitting on the chairs with my whole class made me feel proud. My family sitting up on the bleachers could see where I was sitting because of my shiny letters. I knew my parents had to be the most fulfilled they have ever been because I had achieved a high school diploma. Graduation was something that many doctors did not give my parents hope for those many years ago. I ended up in the top 25% of the class. My mom had tears of joy, rolling-down her eyes as she gave me the biggest hug ever. My family and I went out to eat right after the ceremony. I then got dropped off at an overnight lock-down for a graduation party. Oh boy, that was so awesome. We had lots of games, a pool, and each other to keep busy all night. The party was the last time that I saw my long-standing crush TJ, and it would be the last time our whole class would be together, class of '90.

My mom and I at my high school graduation.

Chapter 6
LIFE-CHANGING EXPERIENCE

I had attended a college course during my last semester in high school. We were transferred by bus to the local college for 2 hours then taken back to high school. The course was a nursing assisting course that my high school offered. All along, I had secretly wished to become a doctor and operate on people; however, I knew that was unreachable. The class was the only opportunity I had to be involved in this field; also, it was fun getting off-campus. In the last two weeks, we had to be at the hospital to observe and do hands-on work. It was exciting for me to be allowed to help and share the load with my friends. At one of these days, I was walking down a hallway when I heard a voice from behind me say, "Cerebral Palsy?" It was a male nurse who asked this question. It turns out that his wife had cerebral palsy, which was pregnant, and was a teacher for the deaf. The news was an eye-opener to me! Could she be a possible role model for my life? I did not think marriage was an option for me, so I jumped at the chance to meet her. My friend was embarrassed, thinking I had just picked up another man's phone number for a date which I was known to do.

Me, on the right, with my friend Leah and a nurse during our Nurse Assistant class in high school.

On the day I met Penny, her husband, Chuck, (the nurse), came to pick me up by himself. It seemed odd that my parents let me go with him alone. When we arrived at their house, I saw a blonde, green-eyed beautiful lady sitting in a wheelchair. She also grew up with Cerebral Palsy, but her speech was unaffected, and yet she used a wheelchair. We talked about our shared past experiences in how we struggled with our disability. It was not long after this meeting that we found out we had a friend in common. Angie was a college friend of my brother that I had met at parties. We all became best of friends over a short time. I saw Chuck lovingly helping Penny with any small thing she needed and carrying her in and out of the car with a smile.

Their home always felt so peaceful and full of joy that it made me wondered what made them act this way. Two weeks after we met, they started talking to me about Jesus Christ, the Son of God, who died for our sins so we can one day be with our loving Father in heaven. They told me about God's grace and mercy towards us and on how He is always there and never forsakes us. These words made me feel warm and fuzzy inside and gave me a different perspective from what the Catholic Church had ever showed me. I was thirsty to hear more words of truth of what the bible had to say about Jesus. The moment of truth happened when they asked if I wanted to repeat the sinner's prayer by confessing my sins, repenting, and accepting Jesus into my heart. WOW, what a rush of emotions I felt that all I did was to break down crying out of gratitude and happiness knowing that Jesus forgave me!

My friendship with Penny blossomed as the weeks went by. We went to church together, I saw how happy she lived a married life with her disability, and she taught me how to read and understand the bible. Of course, I did have problems with my family about me changing "religion," but I felt the happiest at church than I had ever been. I learned that becoming a Christian is not about replacing a religion; it is about having a personal relationship with Jesus and no other. I was also able to witness Penny's pregnancy and safe delivery of her daughter. Penny's friendship gave me tremendous hope that I can have a family of my own someday!

I started at our community college that fall with high expectations and a sense of freedom. I joined several social clubs to keep myself busy. I enjoyed going out with friends to night clubs or hosting parties at my house like any other young adult. By this time, I was a back-sliding and immature Christian. The term means that while I was still going to church regularly, I was not behaving in such a way to show that I had become a new creation in Christ Jesus.

I did date sporadically, but it was mostly in groups of either my friends or my brothers' friends. I attracted older men, and that was a fun challenge for me. I enjoyed dating and partaking in the Spring Break nightlife. I might have put myself in dangerous situations where I could have ended raped or killed at least five times. In some of my dates, we would end up alone or far away from the crowd, where no one would know where we were. With my disability, it was easy for a man to overpower me to do whatever he wanted. Thankfully, every man treated me with respect when I said the word, No. After several years, I realized that God's mighty hand was always protecting me.

I am incredibly proud of my parents. The lack of education did not prevent them from getting ahead in life. In 14 years, they opened and operated five businesses. The first and main one was our lumber yard. Mom and dad worked side by side to make this business thrive. Then, my dad opened two tortilla factories supervised by a trusted family member. My mom wanted to have her achievement; therefore, she opened a booming flower shop. My mother's plant knowledge made it useful when operating her flower shop. Lastly, they opened a high-end restaurant with tasty cuisine. I was too young and not able to provide any help with the businesses. The inability to help made me feel sad because I wanted to be a useful member of my family. I saw my parents working late at home on the accounting or forecasting aspects of the companies, which made me feel proud of them because realizing how far they got with only a seventh-grade education. It is because of my parents' work ethic and dedication that I also strive to put out my best!

I insisted my parents send me to driving school. I did not know if I was going to be able to drive, but I was willing to give it a try! It took months to convince them to let me do it; however, they finally cave in. I took the regular driving classes with other students and also the actual driving hours log too. After a couple of months of training, I took the driving test and passed on the first try. I was so ecstatic and relieved I had passed that I started daydreaming about what car I would get. Unfortunately, my parents were very stern with me about not driving at all because they did not want to see me one day in an accident or death. I was not happy about that decision but thrilled about what I did accomplished.

Chapter 7
A New Beginning

In early 1993 my parents were in the middle of a divorce. I did not want to be at my house anymore, seeing my mother's pain and any other drama unfold. I decided to apply to the University of Texas in San Antonio. In the past two years, I had asked my dad to let me go to UTSA, but he did not agree. I saw this time as my window of opportunity. I applied, and in April, I received my acceptance letter. I was so ecstatic I could not believe I was finally going! I sought help with the Texas Rehabilitation Commission, and they paid for all my tuition plus room and broad. It was a fantastic offer I could not resist, and I was not going to let my dad decide for me anymore. I thought my summer was going to be carefree in anticipation of preparing for my move in the Fall, but God had other plans.

It was in June of 1993 when I met my future husband at a night club called Genesis. That name would become ironic later on as meeting Ozzy would be a new beginning in my life. The description might sound very corny, but our encounter happened this way. I was at the club with a group of five girls sitting at a table opposite the front door. I always liked to see the new people coming in for the night. Then I noticed a strangely dressed young man coming through the door. June in Brownsville is in the upper 90's, so when I saw him with a white turtle neck, blue jeans shorts, and a baseball cap, he caught my interest. He passed by my table a couple of times, and then he surprised me from behind. Ozzy asked me if I wanted to dance; however, my dilemma was that all my friends were out on the dance floor, and I was watching the purses. I told him why I could not go dance, so his response was, "Ok, my name is Oswaldo, but my friends call me Ozzy. If you want to dance with me later, I'll be by the pool tables," Any other guy would have felt rejected and will not ask you again, but he did. So, deer devil me, I went later on to talk and dance with him. My friends all thought I was crazy for going up to him; however, we danced for the rest of the night.

Ozzy's version on the way he saw me is sweet. He says, "As I entered into the club, I saw you across the crowded room in your hot pink dress looking around with your big brown eyes. I knew that I had to talk to you. My older brother told me not to go to you because he knew you were disabled, but that made me want to meet you more." We stayed together until the club closed. My friend Patty and I met Ozzy for an early breakfast. We hit it off so well together that we exchanged phone numbers. He told me that he had gotten out of the Marines 2 weeks prior after serving eight years. That night I got home super late, but no one heard me come in. Ozzy and I went out every week to the beach, the movies, the night clubs, or go out to eat. One day when we went out for lunch, I was eating a piece of meat when Ozzy made me laugh so hard that outshoots the piece of meat right next to his head! I was so embarrassed that I wanted to crawl under the table, but he was gracious and pretended nothing happened. Ozzy was very attentive to my needs. If I needed my food cut, or help down the stairs, or open the car door, he was there for me!

It was getting close to my move to UTSA, but it became bittersweet. I was getting my independence from my family, but now I had to leave a great guy behind. My mom, my friend Danny, and I drove off to San Antonio with my belongings. We got to set up my dorm room while I met my roommate. I was so surprised to see how much alike we were in our personalities that it felt like we already knew each other. Mom spent three days on campus, getting familiar with my school routine. A state program paid a student in the dorms of my choosing to be my provider. Jackie was an out-going and sweet girl who went in the mornings to help me get dressed, do my hair, and get me ready for the day. At night she checked up on me, and she straightened up my room. Jackie and I became friends for life. Also, another sweet friend for life is Cindy, whom I met later that semester in a Christian club in school. That old saying is true: "The friends you meet in college stay friends for life."

~ Cindy and I remained friends all of our lives. After I was married, we would see each other once a week. She became like an aunt to my kids, always giving them gifts and also correcting them. She was my prayer partner throughout our friendship, and we would hang out at the mall, drink coffee, and catch up with our weekly activities. She turned out to be my trusted best friend. ~

I had so many fun adventures living in the dorms and also fun meeting Christian people my age enjoying life without alcohol. I stayed at UTSA for two semesters, and I loved it. Ozzy would visit me sometimes, but it would get harder to say goodbye every time he left. I decided to go back home one year later. I did not want to look like a failure, but for the first time, I put my pride aside. Ozzy and I dated and had our big adventures for two years until we got engaged.

We got married on July 6, 1996, at South Padre Island, like I always wanted. The intimate ceremony was right along the ocean where the music player failed, but our guests started to sing the wedding march for us, and that made it even sweeter. We had a 200 guests' celebration at the hotel pus a big surprise. My husband sang a song for me by Eric Clapton, "You Look Wonderful Tonight." I felt in a dream because I never allowed myself to imagine that I would someday be married.

My dream wedding.

Chapter 8

MY MIRACLE BABIES

I did not want to live in a small town anymore, so we moved to San Antonio to have more job opportunities. My mom had moved here after the divorce; therefore, we moved into the apartment with her. It was in November when we found a church that we liked. I had never heard of Calvary Chapel; however, Ozzy attended them in California. They are a non-denominational spirit-filled church where they teach verse by verse through the bible. It was like someone had thrown a bucket of cold water on me because attending this church made the Word of God come alive. Nonetheless, it still took us several years to become mature Christians. ~We would have never known that even after 22 years we would still attending the same church.~

Early in 1998, we started to think about having a baby. I never wanted to have babies because I assumed I could not handle them, and kids did not understand my disability. I visited my Neurologist for advice before trying to get pregnant. To my surprise, the doctor gave me discouraging information. He said not to get pregnant at all because the medicine that I take can have several health risks for the baby. I take anti-seizer medicine that may cause a cleft lip, cleft palate, or Spinal Bifida to a baby. I knew this in my teenage years, but hearing it now had a different importance. I went home disappointed, crying to my husband that I could not give him a baby. He patiently calmed me down and reaffirm that doctors are not gods that know a certain future. It is only

Jesus who is really in control of our future. We decided to pray and wait on the Lord for guidance. One night, while I was praying for comfort, I heard a scripture pop up in my mind. Psa 37:4 Delight yourself also in Jehovah, and He shall give you the desires of your heart. I took it to heart and trusted in the Lord on His promise.

A couple of months later, I was pregnant! We were so happy that Ozzy was going to every check-up, and I was enjoying a comfortable pregnancy. I never had morning sickness or any craving, but I did eat all my food now. At this point, Ozzy and I were still busy going to UTSA. At my 5-month check-up (June 9th) I was going to have an ultrasound at the hospital to see the baby. We arrived excited and nervous with high expectations to see the image of our baby. The doctor laid me on the table and rubbed the stethoscope on me, and then the room became silent. We could hear a pin drop. The doctor sat down to tell us there was no heartbeat showing. The fetus had died two weeks prior according to their measurements. We heard the words, but we could not understand what it meant for us. We left the hospital in gloom spirits only to sit at a restaurant and digest what had happened. My mom was coming home from out of town later that day, so Ozzy and I laid in bed together comforting each other. God's grace is sufficient for us was the only thing that kept coming to our minds.

It was not easy knowing I had a dead baby in my tummy for two days until I had my DNC done at the hospital. The doctor gave me something to provoke my body to go into labor. It took 6 hours of pain-free labor when my baby slipped out. Ozzy did not want me to hold him, so I would not get traumatized. Nevertheless, I needed to embrace my baby. He was going to be a boy, so we named him Little Ozzy. He would hang off from the palm of our hands because he was only eight inches long. I cradled him for about 10 minutes until Ozzy took him out of my arms. I asked Ozzy to at least take a picture of our son for his memory book I was preparing. It was hard going home empty-handed, but we had our church praying for healing and comfort. I could not understand why this happened; nonetheless, I knew Jesus had allowed this for a purpose.

Sometimes we see that purpose later in life, but other times God will reveal it to us when we see Him face to face in Heaven. The strange thing I was heartbroken, but I did not cry until it was my birthday. I had already imagined that on my birthday I should have had a big belly and it was not there. I cried until I released all of my emotions.

In November, God had blessed me with another pregnancy. Yes, we were happy, but a piece of my innocence was lost. Everything was easy going, but I had that cautious worry in the back of my mind. Being cautious did not mean I did not trust the Lord, not at all, but my mind was guarding my heart against any other hurts or disappointments. I kept going to school and going to church to grow in my faith. Since Ozzy worked nights, he was always too tired to go to church Sunday mornings. I would take the Via Trans (public transportation for disabled) to church, and then my pastor's wife would drive me home. The ride was a 30 minutes drive one way, and I never heard Joanne (pastor's wife) complain. She had a servants' heart. It was on all these rides where Joanne and I had our intercessory prayers for Ozzy. We prayed for him for the next seven years until he finally recommitted himself to Jesus.

I had already stopped drinking and going out with my husband before my first pregnancy, but he continued. On Friday, he went out to a bar for a couple of drinks while I stayed at home. When one in the morning came around, I was mad because he was not home yet, but when 3 and 4 in the morning rolled around, I was scared. I would call his cell phone every 15 minutes to no avail. My mom got up at 5 am to go to work. When she noticed Ozzy's car was not there, she asked me where he was. I could not give her an answer, and she said a comment that shocked me. Mom said, "I hope he is with another woman and not in jail." I could not believe my ears. I had been praying all night for help when the phone rang at 8 am. It was Ozzy calling from jail. He had gotten a DWI and hence needed somebody to pick him up and pay the bail bond. We did not have any other family member here and no cash on hand I did not know who to call. I called Pastor Jim, all embarrassed and ashamed. Jim, with his love and grace, did not hesitate to go for

Ozzy as soon as possible. The rapid response taught us that no matter what we do, Jesus is always there to receive us with open arms. The incident made Ozzy stop drinking and smoking from that very day.

On my 5th month of pregnancy, we went to the hospital for our 1st ultrasound. Ozzy had a test at school, so my mom took me to the appointment. Hallelujah, we saw a steady heartbeat on the monitor. Then I noticed the doctor become quiet while she did the body measurements. My doctor left the room and came back with two other doctors. I saw an all too familiar worried expression on their faces. They explained the size of the head, neck, and kidneys was too enlarged. They sadly reported that these were the classic symptoms of a baby with Down Syndrome. I felt my heart drop, and my dreams shattered again. I wished my mom had not been there to hear this hard reality from the doctors, but it was unavoidable. My doctor wanted me to talk with my husband about some options we can do to determine if my baby boy had Down Syndrome for sure.

Mom drove me from the hospital to school to meet up with Ozzy. As soon as I entered the building, it was a Divine appointment, he came down the stairs and immediately knew something was wrong. The halls were empty, so we embraced, and I started crying as I told him what the ultrasound had shown. We went home, thought about it, prayed about it, and talked to the doctor again. We decided not to do any more tests because the amniocentesis test can cause a miscarriage. We agreed that whatever God sends us, we will love him. We talked to our church about the baby, and for four months, the whole church prayed for him. Ozzy told me later what his secret prayer was; "Lord heal him not for me but Norma." We had already picked a great biblical name for him. His name is Elijah, which means "Jehovah is God"! We prayed and had confidence that Elijah was in God's hands.

July 24, 1999, was the 1st proudest moment of my life. I gave natural birth after only 5 hours of labor to my Elijah. I had peace throughout the whole delivery that I did not even think of what might have been. He looked healthy with all ten fingers and toes, but with the health concerns, they whisked him away for observations. I did not see him until 6 hours later until doctors performed all the tests. He did not have any signs of having Down Syndrome, but he did have minor kidney issues. We could not stop praising God after that news. After we brought Elijah home, I was afraid I was not going to be able to care for him by myself while mom and Ozzy were at work. With God's grace, I was able to breastfeed and carry him. Dipper changes were a little tricky. I would get my hands all dirty, but my baby would be clean. I was only able to breastfeed by laying down with him, which I did five months. After his 1st birthday, the doctor checked his kidney problem and said it was all gone. A clean bill of health is yet another answered prayer from our Heavenly Father.

My baby Elijah.

Throughout all these years of my pregnancies and raising our baby, Ozzy and I kept going to UTSA and struggling with work, school, and finding time to do homework. It was tough; however, we managed to enjoy ourselves by taking some business classes together. I graduated with a Bachelor's in Accounting after 11 years of going to school. My son Elijah was two years old when it happened. It took me that long because I could only handle two classes per semester. It took me so long to finish, but I never wanted to give up this dream. My husband graduated two years after I did with a Bachelor's in Business. ~In hindsight, friends tell me what I did here is a miracle because any non-disabled person in this situation would quit school because the pressures were too high. I figured that once I leave school, there would never be a chance to finish later. From this experience, I tell young people to go to college before getting married.

My UTSA Graduation.

Mom and dad were tremendously proud of me.

My husband was very proud of me too.

Like in every marriage, we all have our ups and downs throughout time. We had a very personal trial in ours where if we did not have our personal relationship with Jesus, we could have ended up in divorce. We were both getting mature in our spiritual walk that we knew to turn to the elders of our church for help. By the elders telling us about their own experience, we were able to forgive each other and move forward to be stronger in our marriage because of this test of faith. At the end of the trail, Jesus reminded me He had given me a gift to share. The Lord gave me a verse which became my favorite during any trial. It is in 2Cor 1:4 He comforting us in all our trouble, so that we may be able to comfort those who are in every trouble, through the comfort with which we are comforted by God. It means that the way I felt compassioned by Jesus through someone else, I should take that experience and use it to reassure others.

Summer of 2002, the Lord blessed me with one more pregnancy. We decided to have another baby before I tried to get a job with my new degree. I always wanted to have a little girl since the 1st time, and I secretly prayed for that to happen. I then remembered the scripture the Lord had given me four years ago. Psa 37:4 Delight yourself also in Jehovah, and He shall give you the desires of your heart. I made this into a personal prayer because I knew this would be my last baby since I was already 31 years old. The health risks of being older and the risk complications due to my medicine made us decided to close the baby factory.

February 27, 2003, was the 2nd proudest moment of my life. I gave birth to a healthy and wide-eyed little girl. Natania means "God's gift," and she sure is a beautiful gift from my Lord. Both of my deliveries were 5 hours long, naturally without an epidural, and big 8 lbs. babies. My home life was to live to take care of my babies. I could tell from the start that she was going to be a strong girl. As she grew up, my prediction came true. She was sure a tough girl all her life! I would joke with my husband, saying; "The Lord had a sense of humor when He answered my prayer for a little girl."

My little girl and I playing.

Chapter 9

Raising My Kids

Many people thought my children would have a speech problem since I have one myself. People thought my babies were going to mimic my pronunciations and have their phonics wrong. I wanted to prove to myself and others that having my Cerebral Palsy was not going to interfere in my children's development. I was going to try my best to overcome my limitations to give them an equal start as the other kids. The daily care of my kids was never easy to do. Something that would take other moms 5 minutes to do would take me 20 minutes to accomplished, but it was ok because I was doing it on my own and for my kids. Once again, by the grace of God, my kids spoke by 10 and 11 months old in 3-word sentences. I gave all my time at home to my kids in talking to them, in showing them educational cartoons and repeating the words, and counting and saying the ABC's since they were three months old. I even have home videos of me doing this with them. I had learned that nothing is impossible with Jesus.

As my kids grew up and started school, I made a promise to myself that in whatever school activity they were participating, I would always be there. It was tricky to find a ride because of mom and Ozzy were working. I would somehow manage to find a ride with friends. My kids are the pride and joy of my life. I know God gave them life, yet He allowed me to be part of it. He let me experienced motherhood with all the wonders and struggles that come with it. I am eternally grateful for

In Spite of My Disability

that chance. My kids are the reason I get up in the morning and gladly struggle with my limitations to give them a good quality of life. I want them to know that their mother is a fighter that will not give up easily. I desire that my kids see my example and mimic my behavior when it comes to living their own lives.

My kids were growing up.

2007 By this time, my evenings were full of helping my kids with their homework, playing and talking with them, and struggling during bedtime. They would tire me out but I reminded myself that it was a privilege God had given me. I had a little more time to myself during the day. In the mornings, I had a provider to help me with my personal care, cleaning, and washing my clothes. Once she left, I would wash my kids' clothes or clean their rooms before I would quiet down to read and study the bible. I did not realize that God would use these quiet times to strengthen my faith for something big down the road.

While my kids were babies and were in elementary, I was not evolved so much in church because of babysitting problems and Ozzy working late. My mom always helped me during the day. I did not want to ask her for any more help at night. I missed the fellowship with other women, but we all have different seasons throughout our lives. My season right now was raising my kids and teaching them to love the Lord. The seclusion did not come easy since I had been a social butterfly. I missed the face to face interactions, giggling, and hugging with each other. A simple touch from a friend is always effective medicine for a hurting or lonely woman. My pastor's wife would remind me to submerge myself in the Word so that I could be capable of when the fiery darts from the enemy would come my way. I can stand firm! As a mom with young kids, I had to fight for that quiet time. If not, I would find myself short-tempered and without much joy from the Lord. A quick 10 minutes bible reading fixed that right away.

As the kids got older and played together more, I was able to reestablish myself into the women's ministry. We have met for this ministry on Monday nights for 13 years now. We would do some worship, pastor's wife would teach a study, and ending with wonderful individual fellowship. The fellowship gave young moms a chance to be ministered to by the older and wiser moms or the single ladies to be encouraged too. After leaving the studies, we all felt our faith lifted and ready to face the week with God's help.

Chapter 10
New Opportunities

Throughout these years, I would attend an annual Women's Retreat held in different areas around San Antonio. These were our highlights of the year because the women got pampered on these weekend getaways. They were usually out in the Hill Country, where the beautiful nature surrounded us. The campsite would prepare all meals and indulge us with great snacks in between Bible studies. Nighttime was especially fun because we would share our intimate thoughts and fears. We also shared our past failures and victories in our faith. We all experienced a mountain-top feeling with the Lord at some point during the retreat. We were all sad knowing we had to leave that closeness with Jesus and face the day to day trails again.

It was around 2013 after our Monday night study my pastor's wife talked with me and told me she saw a growth in my faith and wanted to give me a chance in ministry. I was shocked! Joanne had allowed me to teach on biblical marriage issues once a month in our Monday night's study. I was very nervous, but yet again, God's grace gave me the strength to speak in front of a group. I can be very outgoing and talkative. When I have to talk to more than four people, my speech becomes difficult to understand because I get nervous. I taught for one year, and that showed me I could depend on Jesus for everything. ~I realized this was what God prepared me for all those years when my young kids were at school, and I had those long quiet times in my bible.~

2015 Although I have always desired to go to work and feel like a productive citizen, my first job was to raise my children. My son was about to graduate high school, and my daughter was in middle school when I was offered the job to be our church secretary/bookkeeper. I was delighted and eager to start! I was proud to finally use my knowledge that I had obtained from my college degree those 14 years ago. Mrs. Joanne was very patient with me to bring me up to date on all the bookkeeping methods. I could not stop rejoicing that I had a job in something I liked doing. The offer was only a part-time job since our church has always been small but quaint. Throughout the years, I had been searching, applying, and interviewing for other jobs, but it seems that the Lord wants my time to be free for Him. ~I have heard it said and believe it's true that most disabled workers will be more committed and work harder than their counterparts. I will continue to look for a full-time job until someone allows me to show my abilities. ~

In May of 2016, I lost my dad to an 8-year battle with ALS. "ALS is the loss of the brain to initiate and control muscle movement. With voluntary muscle action progressively affected, people may lose the ability to speak, eat, move, and to breathe." This progression was slow and very sad to see a once vibrant, energetic man that he was. The hardest year was the last year of his life. My dad did not want to admit his body was failing him. He would still try to walk to the bathroom and fall. The only one at home during the day was mom and me. That meant we had to muster up strength beyond our abilities to lift a 170 lbs body. The situation was not safe for anyone. Mom called the ambulance because he could not help us anymore. After a month in the hospital, he entered a nursing home where he had to eat blended food and could not walk or talk anymore. Mom, my daughter, and I sat at his bedside when my dad passed away. The one thing I was happy about was that he always recognized us. Two days before he died, he kept giving my mom kisses.

By this time, my husband and I had been Children Ministry Directors for four years. In the Summer of 2017, we hosted our 1st VBS in many years. The program was my first one organizing it as the head director with a whole new curriculum. I set my mind to learn all the different aspects of it, and with lots of prayer and many meetings with all the volunteers, God made it a memorable time. We had lots of challenges like the no air condition for that week and having to move locations right after VBS. The struggle of the unbearable heat was worth watching the neighboring children learn about Jesus. It was awesome to watch how God made each of us move in unison to accomplish His propose. We hosted another one the following year in our brand-new location where God gave us a clean and beautiful setting. That VBS week was also a great succus!

In the Fall of 2017, my son Elijah started going to UTSA, my alma mater, and it was fun going to the campus with him to show him around. I was proud that one of my kids got to go there. It is never easy to let your child grow up right in front of your eyes, but we need to trust God that He will direct their paths.

My daughter, Natania, entered high school, and I was excited for her since I had a great time in high school. I was hoping she would join clubs and events at school; however, it tuned out to be the opposite. She hung out with the wrong group of kids. She then became a significant challenge in our lives. Without disclosing too much, she did the typical teenage rebellion. I had to remind myself of a verse in 1 Corinthians 10:13 "No temptations has taken you but what is common to man; but God is faithful, who will not allow you to be tempted above what you are able, but will make a way to escape, so you may be able to bear it." The verse meant that I was not alone in this struggle. Many other parents have gone and will continue to go through similar situations. God's mercy will not let any conflict be too extreme for you to drown in your sorrows. He will always give you a hope and a way to change that situation. I continually had to remind myself of this promise because without God, I do not think I would have come out victorious.

It took about six tortious months for her to get back on track and start behaving like her usual self. It was difficult because I had to stay silent. I did not want to share it with my family because I felt ashamed.

I could not share at church because the fear of being judged was there. There were two ladies I did share my struggles with whom they prayed with me the whole time. It was challenging to see your daughter digging herself into a pit where you could not save but had to let God do His will. I wish I can tell you what all she did, but it is not my place. It is going to be part of her testimony one day!

2018 In spite of all the struggles, we were able to give Natania a Mexican Quincenera just like I had many years ago. The ceremony is a celebration of a young girl growing up to be a young lady in society's eyes. My mother and I planned everything, and by the kindness of family and friends, we were able to give Natania a traditional party. I missed my dad being here because he loved parties and traditions. My pastor led a short ceremony, followed by a dance. It was nice to be surrounded by so many family and friends that I enjoyed dancing with my husband most of the night. It felt surreal to me that my life had come a full circle, that I was now the mother of the party girl instead of me being- the party girl!

My daughter's Quincenera.

My mom has always been at my side from growing up to taking care of my babies to helping teaching them how to drive. Most people did not know her name because she was known as "Norma's mom." The unfamiliarity never bothered her; she was happy putting me in the spotlight. My mom has always been very petty and youthful throughout her life. I can not imagine my life without her enormous help. Even though we still live together, we live our own lives. It is great to be able to celebrate with her every holiday and any accomplishment a family member does. It is with her strong will and strict upbringing that I am the woman I am today!

In July 2018, we celebrated our 23rd wedding anniversary! Like I said before, not in a million years, I would had dreamed I would have married at all much less for this long. In my youth, if I had heard of a couple married these many years, I would have thought that was a boring old couple. But now, I feel like we are just starting to have fun! My son is halfway through college and hopefully out of the house soon. My daughter is a sophomore in high school with ideal grades and better behavior. What more can I ask? I have plans for when we will become Empty Nesters and ready to do fun stuff for ourselves.

We are celebrating our 23rd wedding Anniversary.

Closing

I have desired to write this book ever since high school, but life happened. It took me eight years to finish writing this book. It sounds like a long time; nevertheless, it was not continuous writing. Sometimes I would write every day or one week per month. I even got writer's block for a year because I was afraid to finish the book, imagine that! I want to educate and encourage parents and their kids with disabilities that there is no limit to what we can do! Given the right therapy and resources, we can obtain our self-independence through the help of our loved ones. My dream, after this book, is to receive invitations to inspire groups and organizations with my life's story. I like to see people's smiles when they can imagine their child do some of the things I have done. I am also going to keep on applying for jobs in the accounting field or related fields in hopes someone will give me a chance to show myself.

My life has been full of highs and lows like everyone else. The main reason I have not fallen into a deep depression is because of my personal relationship with Jesus. When we believe that Jesus is God the Father and the creator of all things, we have no reason to fear. We can put our whole trust in Him knowing He is a Sovereign God and that He will always have our best interest in mind. When bad things come our way, we should look up and pray for guidance. He is a faithful and a just God who will forgive our sins the moment we ask Him too! Trusting God is how I have lived my adult life and believing that He will work out every situation in my life according to His perfect Will no matter how bad it looks!

In Spite of My Disability

God has blessed me all my life. Some may say, but you have a disabled body that does not work correctly! In spite of my disability, I have done many things! I have come to accept that God gave me a perfect body and mind to achieve his purposes. For as many lives that I have touched knowingly and unknowingly, it is worth being limited but being used by God. I will not tell you it has been easy because it has not! One has to make their determination if to whether to feel sorry for yourself or to fight against adversity and do something in your life. If we choose to fight the obstacles in our lives, we will know the sweet taste of victory and live a happy and productive life!

Friend's Comments

Norma's determination not to let her physical challenges limit her ability to achieve her aspirations and goals is a great encouragement to never give up in the face of obstacles. God has blessed her with a faith in Him that enables her to be an overcomer knowing she is always in the palm of His hand. Her faith shines brightly and helps others to trust in God.
Joanne

You befriend many ladies, are a good listener, are a faithful friend, you have unbelievable confidence in God, you are a triumphant prayer warrior, hold a job outside your home, and smile nearly all the time.
Dorothy

I remember what a good dancer you are. I remember you would not let your disability get the best of you and control your life. I remember you would try something and not give up on it until you were able to conquer it. I also recall your mother used to Velcro your pants to make it was easy for you to put them on and take them off.
Lisa

Norma, you inspire me even though I don't see you often. You have strong faith and determination. I perceive no disability when I talk to you. Just a resilient Christian.
Patty

You are an amazing woman! I admire you so much! You're a wife and mother, I admirer your strength to conquer the things in life! You are a woman of God! You have such a sweet spirit about you! I feel blessed you are my friend, an amazing lady!
Angela R

www.ingramcontent.com/pod-product-compliance
Ingram Content Group UK Ltd.
Pitfield, Milton Keynes, MK11 3LW, UK
UKHW022220230426
12048UKWH00016BA/971